MELTWATER

ALSO BY CLAIRE WAHMANHOLM

Redmouth
Wilder

MELTWATER

poems

CLAIRE WAHMANHOLM

MILKWEED EDITIONS

Published 2023 by Milkweed Editions
Printed in Canada
Cover design by Tijqua Daiker
Cover photo by rawpixel.com / Jack Anstey
Author photo by Daniel Lupton

Library of Congress Cataloging-in-Publication Data

Names: Wahmanholm, Claire, author.
Title: Meltwater : poems / Claire Wahmanholm.
Description: First Edition. | Minneapolis : Milkweed Editions, 2023. | Summary: "A haunting collection that inhabits a disquieting future where fear is the governing body, "the organ and the tissue / and the cell, the membrane and the organelle.""-- Provided by publisher.
Identifiers: LCCN 2022028468 (print) | LCCN 2022028469 (ebook) | ISBN 9781639551019 (trade paperback) | ISBN 9781639551026 (ebook)
Subjects: LCGFT: Poetry.
Classification: LCC PS3623.A35648 M45 2023 (print) | LCC PS3623.A35648 (ebook) | DDC 811/.6--dc23
LC record available at https://lccn.loc.gov/2022028468
LC ebook record available at https://lccn.loc.gov/2022028469

Milkweed Editions is committed to ecological stewardship. We strive to align our book production practices with this principle, and to reduce the impact of our operations in the environment. We are a member of the Green Press Initiative, a nonprofit coalition of publishers, manufacturers, and authors working to protect the world's endangered forests and conserve natural resources.

CONTENTS

MELTWATER

O

Once there was an opening, an operation: out of which oared the ocean, then oyster and oystercatcher, opal and opal-crowned tanager. From ornateness came the ornate flycatcher and ornate fruit dove. From oil, the oilbird. O is for opus, the Orphean warbler's octaves, the oratorio of orioles. O for the osprey's ostentation, the owl and its collection of ossicles. In October's ochre, the orchard is overgrown with orange and olive, oleander and oxlip. Ovals of dew on the oat grass. O for obsidian, onyx, ore, for boreholes like inverted obelisks. O for the onion's concentric Os, observable only when cut, for the opium oozing from the poppy's globe only when scored. O for our organs, for the os of the cervix, the double Os of the ovaries plotted on the body's plane to mark the origin. O is the orbit that cradles the eye. The oculus opens an O to the sky, where the starry outlines of men float like bubbles between us and oblivion. Once there were oarfish, opaleyes, olive flounders. Once the oxbows were not overrun with nitrogen. O for the mussels opening in the ocean's oven. O for the rising ozone, the dropping oxygen, for algae overblooming like an omen or an oracle. O Earth, outgunned and outmanned. O who holds the void inside itself. O who has made orphans of our hands.

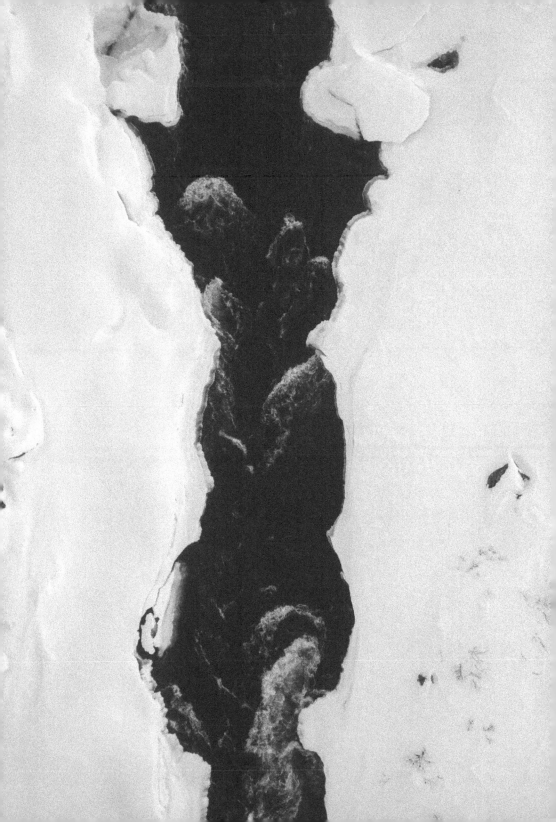

HUNGER

Wolf that I was,
I had no names

for the different shades
of hunger—the green

ache of one versus
the pink pang of another,

the sharper edges
versus the softer.

All I knew was need,
the opening of

possibility, a way
to be full. Belly-down

in the field, I watched
this new hunger with

my predator's eye—
the way it rippled

like rain showers
across the grass,

the way it sprang
to the sky, dragging

its colors behind it.
Wolf that I was,

I watched it like
prey, but it wasn't.

It wasn't a hunger
for tearing or blood,

though it would be
later. In the sky

it breathed clouds
into the shape

of smaller wolves—
slow and whole, or

leggy and quick,
shredding as they ran.

The kind of hunger
that would fit

an entire body
inside it.

When I nuzzled
the clouds, my snout

came back cold.
I slunk through

the woods, empty
and dreaming.

In my hunger,
every little voice

could have been
a daughter, every

hooded shadow.
In my dreams,

I swallowed clouds
that hardened into

stones. My body was
an infinite well to drop

infinite stones into,
a belly to slit open

and stitch shut.
In those dreams,

the knife does not
even wake me up.

YOU WILL SOON ENTER A LAND WHERE EVERYTHING WILL TRY TO KILL YOU

. . . into a harbor
Where it all comes clear,
Where island beings leap from shape to shape
As to escape
Their terrifying turns to disappear.
>   GJERTRUD SCHNACKENBERG

Inside me you're an eel, a whipping ghost, a root of sinew leaping
from blackberry to minnow to walnut tree. Your body sleeps
and bucks beneath my body's sheet: only the idea of you
is visible. I pulse with doorknobs that bob then sink back into
the sea of me, ungraspable.
                          Mimicry implies its own necessity:
that you are already prey, and everything out here means you harm.
You are, it does, and I have done nothing to stop it—have, in fact,
done all I can to make it easy for the world to wrap itself around you
and squeeze. I have no plan to keep the chemicals separate
from the lake, the acid separate from the rain, the bird from the glass
that breaks it. Thud. I picture your blood on every brick ledge,
your fingers beneath each sledgehammer. I will imagine your death
in every season—by water in summer, by illness in autumn,
a febrile seizure whenever you close your eyes.
                                    In the world's rich dirt
I could have planted brambles, clovers. I could have just loved
the earth instead of inventing new ways to hurt. Half our genome
is shared with fruit, more with fish, the most with ghosts. Your body
seems to know this—that jawless fish cannot be struck by cars,
that no one mourns a blackberry crushed beneath a naked foot.

Therefore be deep-dwelling muscle. Be sweet vegetable
a moment longer. Before us lies a fatal, blossoming desert, full
of heat and shadow. I am about to set my heart down
into a wild burrow. A clock is about to start.

GLACIER

The room was huge and cold. The glacier's skin smelled like pine, snowcloud, bog, lichen. There were stanchions around the ice so the audience wouldn't touch or lick its weeping face. Some people had brought their children. Our brains stuttered. *Who could ever— What would possess— Who would want—* I didn't like the exposure. Whenever I heard a spurt of knee-high laughter, whenever a child looked up at me thinking I was its mother, I felt stripped of another layer of clothing. Everyone knows that children smell fear, but they smell shame even better. By the time the lights dimmed I was naked and didn't know what to do with my hands and arms. I couldn't cover everything. For an additional five hundred dollars you could mount a ladder and point a hair dryer at the glacier for two minutes. With your gun of hot air you could shape the surface into pits—a gentle divot for an eye, a more forceful one for a mouth. You could make sweat run from armpits, from the small of a slick back. Any meltwater was yours to keep. We had heard that some people had vials from all five glaciers lined up on their mantels like Hummels. Pictures were free but we didn't take any. It felt pornographic—all that melting, all those crowds. One couple recorded their entire session, the machines blinking and blinking, their voices tangling as they narrated. I stared at the ceiling. I rubbed the ticket stub in my pocket until it pilled into pulp. We didn't talk in the car. When we got home I was so thirsty. Like wanting to have sex after a funeral. I stood in the shower and let the water spray haphazardly into my mouth. There was so little I hardly had to swallow. I bent over the sink and cupped my hands to my mouth over and over and over again. I put my mouth directly over the faucet and hummed. This sounds like a metaphor but isn't. I'm just talking about water.

MELTWATER

Ice

        stretches   between

us

        and   history

.

        O

        slushy   shadow

O   long

gray   rain

        that

        floods   the

Ice   with

                                              memory

          the

                                    water of   the

future   followed

          us,   no   ark

                                    appeared

          ,

                                                            no

              spell of   un

          making   .

                        time   is

a   land
                                    of
                    lies   ;

                                    we

                    stumble
between glaciers and memory   and
                                    try

                                                to
explain

                    our   path.

            O   uncommonly sunny
                                                                death

                                that

            brightened

the

summer
            snow.

                              the melting point
of

                  ice
                                    is
                              Empire

      .

      formed by dust
                  ,

      we

                  were

                                    baptized
in

concrete

and

our

own   acceleration

.

it
trickled down   to the

future

in

gray

statistics   O

child

the

meltwater   was   so   deep.

M

M is for murmur and mutter—the ambiguity of the Möbius strip, the marsh, the *maybe* trembling between two membranes. M is for mother, dark matter, the matrix that cradles the muscadine, marble, monosyllable, moon. Be menagerie, multivocal, madrigal. I carry your multitudes through midsummer, through marigolds and mayapples, through mud. I hide you in the middle of a maze, bury you like minerals in the mine of my body. You are marrow-deep, marine, mollusk in your mother-of-pearl hull. The months are a moat between you and melancholy, missiles, mourning. M is for the meteor magnifying through the telescope's lens, the metronome unmuffling. M is for metamorphosis and mutant. I am more and more mountainous. I am a mare rolling in a midnight meadow, all musk and muzzle. M is for the migrations of monarchs, mule deer, mullet, for magnetic fields, for the way the world pulls you from me and you materialize. You are motor made music, machine made mortal. I am mended and marooned somewhere between mist and milk. I molt, am mangled. I molt, am myself.

IN A LAND WHERE EVERYTHING IS ALREADY TRYING TO KILL ME, I ENTER A NEW PHASE OF MY LIFE IN WHICH IT WOULD BE VERY BAD IF I DIED

because now there is a child and her mother is burning
with rapture and terror and has my eyes and teeth.
She is parasite, doppelgänger, and I would die
if she unmothered me. She holds my breath as I pass
a speeding truck. She holds my breath when we see
a mother duck and a duckling that would not know
if she died. We are not that kind. Our kind keens
for a long time and the sadness accumulates in our bodies
like lead or tapeworm eggs. I feel sorry for all of us,
the leaving and the left. Everything is bearing down,
bearing down. For "bereft," make a tearing sound,
which is different from a tearing sound, which is made
behind the face instead of at the base of the throat.
I hold my breath so I can't choke to death. A child
watches me not eat my sandwich. It is my child,
it is my own watchfulness, we are the same kind,
the sandwich is stale, we stare at it balefully.
It would be kind of the world to let us live until
we are tired of it, until it is stale and unpleasurable.
But that is called *heaven*, not *world*. Once I am dead,
I won't know it, but that doesn't help. I already miss living—
all its bells and tulips and feelings. There is *maybe death*
and there is *death death* and that's all. I will spend
the rest of my life *maybe dying* until I actually do.
I have practiced and practiced. I have tried to drive out
the sugar that attracts the sadness. But the mother in me
has fallen in love with everything. I want to tell her

to shut her eyes, to keep her hands in her pockets,
but she must hold the child's hand as she crosses the street.
She must eat if she wants to see the child, which is better
than eating. I have not left her any white stones
to follow out of this forest. There is only the sweet
dangerous darkness and the fire at the end of it.

MELTWATER

the   edge of

the   ocean

rises

slowly toward the

mountain

summit,

meaning

the end of

land

.

is

there   a

word   for

the

gone

land   ,
the   old

          future

      ,
                                                  the former
                                                  time

                      .
          is

      it

a   graph

            is
it

              a document
                  is   it

                          a

                                          map

is

it

a   photograph

,   a   funeral

?

we

melt   under

a thick, fur-like layer

of years.

In Ice   years   ,

                                                              we

                    disappear

          more

                              rapid

                              ly   in

        to

                    the   blue

        .

METAMORPHOSIS WITH MILK AND SUGAR

Every day I pump 84 ounces of milk from my body.
Every day I am filled with, and empty myself of,
the liquid equivalent of a small baby. My eyes sting
as the milk leaves my body. That is the prolactin,
sweetening everything my brain touches. That book
is sweet, those peonies on the table are sweet, the baby
is so sweet that my eyes leak when they brush against her.

I have spent so much time putting so much milk
into the baby that I don't remember when water started
to taste bitter. Like drinking from a hot, reedy pond.
More and more I find myself standing before
the open refrigerator. The milk is 38 degrees and sweet
as ice cream. The faucet rusts over. I cover it
with a dishcloth. I only have eyes for milk.

My brain finds this craving a little too neat,
but that doesn't matter. I am almost always in
the dairy aisle. I am almost always in the parking lot,
lifting the jug to my mouth with both hands.
It blocks out the sun like a sweet cold moon.
I can hear my throat squeezing in my ears as I swallow
and swallow. I imagine myself filling with milk
from the feet up: my ankles cool to the touch,
my knees sweetening, my stomach a marble sea.
When I look at myself in a windshield I see it is real,
I see my face is pearly and trembling.

Though I am made of milk, I can still walk
to the store. I walk very slowly, as if at the bottom
of a swimming pool. I walk slowly so I do not spill.
I am so cold that my eyes fog up when I step outside.
My skin beads like a cold bottle. I am slick in my shoes.

Whenever I see the baby, my eyes frost over
like snow cones. They leave a dusting of sugar on
everything they touch. In my new sugar house, I pick
rock candy grit from the corners of the baby's eyes,
wipe syrup from her nose, brush brown sugar from
her velvet hair. Each night I flick more and more ants
from behind her ears. Each morning more and more
of the baby has disappeared.

IN A LAND WHERE EVERYTHING IS TRYING TO KILL YOU,
I TEACH YOU TO BE AN AUTOTOMIST

I wish someone had taught me years ago. The older you are, the harder it is to part
with yourself like this—to part the hand from the wrist, the lips from
the rest of the face. I don't mean emotionally. I mean the separation is messier,
and hurts. In children, the casting off is clean and, with practice,
painless. I show you the lizard whipping its tail free, the spider unhinging itself
from two of its legs. Together we watch them open
and close across the kitchen floor, blown by an automatic breeze. I tell you
what to expect: tension, then a ripple
of popping—the deep feeling of pulling up a long-rooted weed. Warmth, relief,
numbness for a week, then
terrible itching. But living. It is worth shedding anything for this, I say. I mean it,
mostly. We practice.
You shake your head and your hair drifts through the air, roots and all, bloodless
as cottonwood.
You wave your hand and your nails drop their soft, unfinished moons. Soon
you
will be able to dissolve a faulty organ as easily as deciding to. Snap your fingers
and a fresh one
will inflate into its hollow. The kidnapper will be left gripping a dummy arm,
the tree trunk pinning
a cooling leg. It's true that the new limbs are more fragile. It's true that the numbness
comes back, that spring will feel
less lush on your cheeks, the August rain less electric. It's true that there are patches
of anesthesia in my chest. When I look
toward the stars, I find myself squinting to anchor them onto the sky. But I am alive
to notice the dullness. I am alive to notice the blood
running less redly beneath the flies.

POEM THAT CRIES WOLF

Like all the other poems, it is full of dead children.
Terror-gripped, they have been dropped by the nape on my stoop.
I am relieved to carry them back inside the lines
of my house—I, who have done the gripping, who have been
the wolf. I who am the boy crying for witnesses
against my own rabid imagination. My mind
is a snarl of corners around which death is always
waiting: a wilderness so burgeoning, so over-
run, I cannot see for the lung-pink oleander
sheltering each sharp thing. So the poem is an orchard,
or a house—something gridded into rooms or rows, where
only one version of every possible event
in the universe grows. The death of a child happens
safely here, beneath a dim sunless light, or within
these thinly papered walls. It is pulled down from the clouds
of possibility as if through a lightning rod.
The groundwater carries it cleanly away beneath
the roots of the orchard. I rebuild this dummy house
every night. I close the windows against the tangle
of the actual world, where lightning can strike over
and over without boredom or belief and nothing
is saved. To admit I play this game is to turn on
all the lights and leave the door unlocked. *Come in, come in,*
I have declared myself a believer in magic,
have dared to imagine my children are safe. Outside,
the real moon casts oleander shadows on the wolf,
the wolves, whose blood is my blood, who have been waiting for
the light to strike their eyes, for the door to open wide
enough to finally be unclosable. It happens
now. It has already happened. No one is coming.

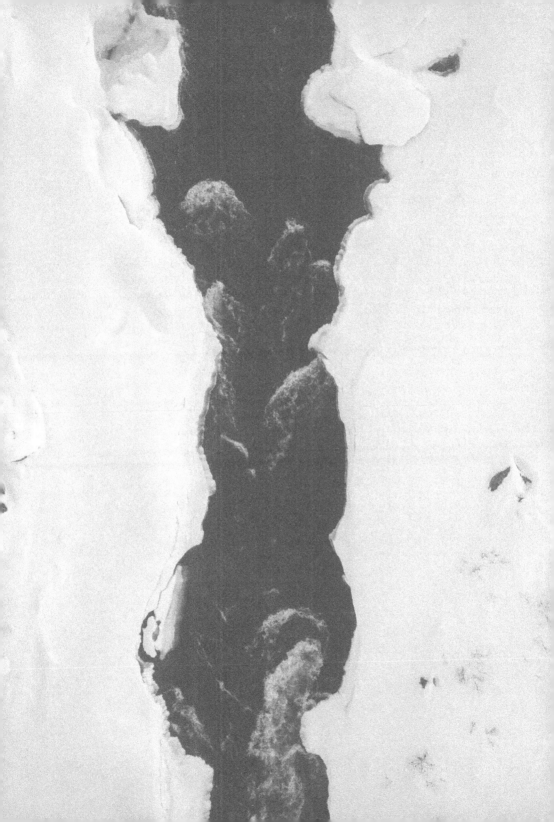

GLACIER

We waited behind the velvet rope. The calving had to happen naturally, or else it was illegal. The way our child was allowed to bring home flowers only if something had already snapped them from their stems. No dynamite, no artificial summering. This meant waiting. Our tickets could only guarantee a weeklong window. We stood for two days before we heard the thunder. Like deep static, or wind against a microphone. We didn't record the ice running like a river of sand, churning into low clouds. We didn't blink at the bright blue undersides turning over and over in the bay. Afterward, my hands were stiff and furred with purple velvet. Fleets of lifeboats towed the smallest ones to shore. I could hear the saws buzzing all night, breaking the calves down into cubes that would snap and jump in our water glasses. I dreamed I lay bedded beneath sheets and sheets of ice. I dreamed of epochs of snow, atmospheres and winds whipping above me by the millions. In the morning the room was full of ragged clouds, washcloth-heavy. When I wrung one out onto my face, I felt like a ghost: ancient, dizzy, almost a hologram. A chunk of topaz sat in my water glass. The bluer the ice, the less air it holds. Like our own faces, our own cold hands dropping stones into the well of the future to see how much deeper it goes. I sipped and the cube flashed like a prism, like floodlights, an interrogation, bright as poison. I tasted the Miocene's kelpy tang, the lonesome chalk of the Pliocene, base notes of bedrock and urchin. The blue bulged in my throat like a sad balloon. I swallowed and swallowed but it wouldn't thaw. I stood outside and pointed my chin toward the sun but the numbness had already reached my lungs. My breath bloomed before me like a sad planet, its latitudes shrinking and blue.

MELTWATER

we   land   in   a
cold valley,

run

into   the valley's
blue
shroud

,

become dead .

as   an

echo   ,

we

pass

                                    from

speech   to

                    reported
                                language

        no
                                        One

                    lived
            to   ask
about

        us
                                            .

we

were

all

dead   to

the glacier

,

the

ice,

the Green   ,

the

mountain

,

the

pollen clouds

, which

ring

in

a   sudden

                                 hurricane

                of   alive   ness

.

                       so

much

   horizon

                                          in

   this

  new

     valley

.

STARLING

The war was born like a sudden winter.

For as long as we could remember,
the sky had been one unending sequence of fluid,
heart-stopping sunsets. Night happened
during the few minutes we rested our eyes.
Each sunrise was ripe as a rainforest.

The minute before the war was born,
we had been facing west. It would be
the last sunset, but we didn't know that yet.

Behind us, something cold unfurled in the sky.
I turned around and felt a quickening,
like a child kicking, but it was too early for that.
Above us, the sky turned inside out
and shed the first locust. It fell like a flake
of green ash, neon against the darkness.
We heard the first explosion.

We knew what happened to children born
during wartime. We had seen the exhibits,
had looked at the pictures without fully
looking. As if the images were stereograms
and by going blank in the eyes we would see
something different—something un-horrible,
a non-trauma, a dolphin, a flower—emerge.

I passed a torpor through my blood like drugs
through a drip. I buried the bulb of your body
deep, the opposite of forcing. We pulled down
our blinds and stapled them to the sills.
We sat very still. Beneath the ice of my skin,
you pressed your frozen ear to the war.
You sprouted feelings like new hands.
Your blood mixed with mine and soured.

I watched other children being born,
watched them lie in the crook of an arm,
upturned on a lap, stretched on a bed.
When they lived, their bodies lengthened like trees.

Still I waited. I watched my own face go gaunt,
haunted. When I looked in the mirror all I saw
was the shoreless face of a dark sea,
the bombs exploding over it like auroras.
I didn't even feel you vanish into the trees,
the branching veins of my body that held no leaves.

Within my own bare arms I sing a song
whose refrain goes, *we thought—we only thought—
we never thought.* The single starling is shot down
and its absence is swallowed by the billowing flock.
The song is tuneless as a river of dry rocks.

MORE RABBITS

The child would like more rabbits. The wind has torn the others in its teeth like so much tissue. We've run out of paper, so we use leaves. We still have our X-Acto blades. We use a steady, firm pressure to cut a clean hole in the rabbit's face, use a steady, firm pressure to free its ears and feet from the leaf. We use sap to glue the leaf-rabbit to the stick and make it hop. *There used to be so many rabbits*, we say to the child as we move the shadow-rabbits back and forth before the firelight. *We used to kill them like they were nothing, like as soon as you buried one, three more would pop out from under the shovel's head.* We have told the stories so well that she's sure she's seen a real one. She practices hopping, tries to wiggle her ears.

The child would like more rabbits. But leaves don't exist anymore, so we use our hands. I can make two kinds of rabbits— one on all fours and one sitting up on its haunches. This is more painful than the shadow puppets. My fingers cramp and the fire leaps out and licks my knuckles but I do it anyway. I do it so often my hands curl into rabbits in my sleep. Sometimes I wake to find they've flung themselves as far as they can from my body and are buried beneath a clump of weeds.

The child would like more rabbits. Our hands are rabbits forever now and hop very slowly in front of the fire and are not enough. And because she's polite, because she thinks we are capable of something more than sitting by the fire and crying, she tries *please. OK*, we say, and unveil the hutch that has always been in the yard. *OK*, we say, and pull out a soft baby bunny from our coat pocket. It hops and hops and the child hops behind it and wiggles her ears and pats it very gently. The rabbit is so small in her palm, its fur so translucent it erases everything it rests on. *Thank you*, she says to the grass beneath her hand.

PRIMER

It is the blight man was born for,
It is Margaret you mourn for.
        GERARD MANLEY HOPKINS

Nothing older than grieving.
Not love nor the lurch of leaving
the ground for the first time. (You
remember someone tossing you
into the air.) This is older
even than that. (You land, colder
from your small fall through space, the sigh
of the air still clinging to your ear.) You lie
where you fell on the brown grass. Why
you, why *grass*? Why not name
everything that's going to die with the same
this, this—a neutral tissue, a moss. Pressed,
each syllable ravels into mist, its weight unguessed
and wet on the blades of your tongue. (For-
lorn, you are grass, soft as what you mourn for.)

THE CHILD PUTS APPLES INTO THE MOUTH OF THE TREE

After we lost the child, a hole appeared between your lungs. At first it was the size of a gasp, an apple, a fist. Then it widened into the size of a plate, a small face. We had read about this sort of thing: after a bad grief, the heart rots and turns on the body, sucking everything into it like a spillway. *Look*, you said one day. You put your hand to the edge of the hole and the tips of your fingers vanished. You put your hand in up to your wrist and pulled back the emptiest fist. I was in the middle of dying, but I pulled myself from the dirt and bent before your chest and looked. Instead of the mesh of your body, instead of the room behind you, I saw a black meadow. Warm wind breathing against my skin. I hadn't thought there would be wind. I hadn't thought there would be anything. That night I dreamed of our child in that black meadow, dropping apples into the hollow of a dead tree. Her hands put apple after apple into the mouth of the tree and came back whole. So it was possible. I could feel her breath on each apple as she held it toward me. The meadow rippled with it. When I woke up I reached out in the dark to make sure you hadn't disappeared without me. When you do, I want you to take my hand.

MELTWATER

O

      world,   from Antarctica to   the Siberian

Sea. O   eastern   mountainsides

.

O

road through

          gray ice

        O   cold

             nest

in

a black

field

O   ice cap   in the shape of

all

the

lessons

we

wanted to

learn

but

didn't   .

O   moss

                                                                    on the boulder
                              surrounded

                                                          by excessive
summer   .

                                                                              o

      ship

                              across the
            deep

      .

THE NEW HORTICULTURE

in our despair we have made
a flowerless earth
                  INGER CHRISTENSEN

There used to be bees.

There used to be a name for those who tended them,
a word for the fear of them, a set of instructions
for how to smoke them out from beneath our eaves.

Now no flowers, no bees.
Now we have a thousand words for the word *green*.
We have filed our eyes to more sharply read the dictionaries
of the field, the shallow sea, the fleets of insectivorous birds
who burn our eyes with the breeze of their chlorine-scented wings.

Now there are more and more carnivores. All night we hear
monkeys eating each other loudly in the fruitless trees.

There is sad green and there is scared green and a green
for dread and one for when we can't get out of bed
in the afternoon. We used to feel nostalgic at the smell
of cut grass, but now the sweet half is gone. Now we feel lonely
and panicked as sirens when we pass a fresh lawn.

Something is being rewound. The wind makes a wobbling sound
as it spirals through the glades of cycads.

Some people still make silk flowers, soft and flawless,
expensively odorless. The rest of us bring pots of waterworts
and mosses to the funerals, clasp savage bunches of horsetails.

We grow unruly beneath the shadows of four-story ferns.
Monkey fur clogs our gutters. Monkey blood sometimes mists
through our screens to speckle our botany books,
propped open so we can imagine the smell of lilac and jasmine.

Somewhere, a clock is ticking. Blame spreads like a bog,
acidic and endless. Someone has deleted one hundred million
years of flowers, has cut the brakes.

Someone has pulled the pins out of the grenades,
the only kind of fruit we can still name.

GLACIER

Zero degrees. We signed waivers agreeing to keep our mouths closed. No yawning, which would raise the temperature of the vault. No coughing. I imagined ice cream, ice water, icicles in my throat. I tried to slow my heart rate by imagining waves on the open ocean, the energy orbiting deeply through a packet of water before setting it back down again. The walls of the vault were curved like a planetarium's, holding together a sky so blue and bright it was depthless, yearless. The bergs were so blue and bright they looked like raspberry shaved ice. They sat behind bomb-proof glass, cored and carved down to their frozen hearts. I wanted to fill my eyes with them. I wanted to be solemn and surprised by how easy that was, how small and neat they were on their velvet-draped pedestals, grouped by country of extraction. Each was named for the first man to put his boots on it—*Hubbard, Moreno, Franz Josef, Lambert*. A wave rose and sank on the ocean. I tried to let these facts build something useful and sad in my brain, but everything was a slush of anxiety. Like reading about wars: the hostile parties, the early invasions, the dates bleeding and bleeding into each other. Everything was made of the same material, the same pressure. Crest and trough. Even now we were in a war I didn't know the name of. Even now bombs were falling above ground. It made sense for us to be hiding down here together. The placards mentioned repatriation, but I knew that when it was over, we would not be reunited with our pillaged, melted bodies. A glass of water will not freeze around an ice cube. The bird calls looped and looped, the artificial pine mist stung my eyes, but I kept them open. I imagined waves on the ocean. Maybe we would be renamed for the first things our eyes touched when we resurfaced. *Snowdrop. Reindeer moss. Fjord*. I wanted to be ready for whatever was left of the world.

APOTROPAEI

ancient Greek deities believed to avert disaster

I have decided that you look like me.
In the smoke of calamity, I want to turn to myself,
who is reasonable, who will sympathize, who knows
that as I fall asleep, I picture my house on fire.
I imagine how I would escape from every room.
I imagine not escaping. I imagine my children not escaping.
I can see the smoke, can close up my throat on command,
can sweat so much my sheets would be the last thing to burn.
You are powerless to turn away a fire or a cancer or a kidnapper
or a knife. But I want you to have my face, so that when I say
there are circumstances under which I would kill myself,
you will understand. You will not stop me from running
my hands over their cool shapes to make sure they are still there,
to make sure this too is a room I could escape.

IN A LAND WHERE EVERYTHING IS TRYING TO KILL ME, I CONSIDER LETTING IT

All I would need to do is stand for too long
beneath its jagged, capable shadow.

All I would have to do is let my skin absorb
that shade until my blood runs at 94 degrees.

Hypothermia is so much warmer than
I thought. The confusion begins here,

the mingling. Every time I walk beneath a tree,
more of me tangles with the breeze that lifts

its leaves, which are always 70 degrees, regardless
of geography. It would be so easy, listening

to this flash inside my brain, this fact
that takes up no more space than the open mouth

of a stoma. 50 microns. Half the width
of a neuron. It would be so easy, the sharpened

blade sliding like wind through whatever
comes within range. I snap my mind away

like a sleeve from an open flame, but the thought
will finish what it started. It will home

like salmon, or whales tracing the aura
of a continent. Like a missile. The wire

has been tripped, the fluids in my ear have risen
into waves by the alarm. How long

have I been standing here. Who is the woman
lying in the shade.

THE SUN, THE SHIP

                                        the sun shone
         As it had to on the white legs disappearing into the green
         Water; and the expensive delicate ship that must have seen
         Something amazing, a boy falling out of the sky,
         Had somewhere to get to and sailed calmly on.
                      W. H. AUDEN

Say I have finally died. Say grief has run
the last grain of me through its fist and I lie
piled and dull beneath its shadow, raw material.

If I could be remade, I would not be.
I am done dragging my leaden shoes
through fields ringed with panic,
done lesioning the soil with my nettled shadow.

Let me choose that inhuman coin
of a sun, or the golden ship flying
beneath it toward what might have been
a meteorite, toward what left no stain,
no frozen monolithic wave.

I am ready to see something amazing—
an explosion, a sudden cancer,
a boy falling out of the sky and into the arms
of the water, any gun—
                          and not run
my mind like trees through a pulper,
wondering when my child's turn will come.

For this I would kill all that is warm
and weak in me. I would flush the rot
until my body rinses clear and calm.

Let me sail on lukewarm currents that offer
no recognition of the bodies that fall
through them, though the spray still hangs
like smoke an inch above the water's face.

MELTWATER

we

are

joined

to

crisis

.

We

turn toward

its name
    as

if

it

had chosen
us   .

for   it   ,

we

shine

.

we

part

the

ice sheets

and

count

each   ring

,

sing

death

in

to

the   ear

of the   sea

,   break

the

Ice

into lace.

AT THE END WE TURN INTO TREES

After we lost the child, it became too painful to have a face. Mine had eyes that kept showing me *not her, not her.* There she wasn't in the garden, there she wasn't in the crib, the park. Why hadn't those places erased themselves along with everything she had ever touched. I wanted every map to be lace, wanted atlases to crumble between their covers, for the cut-out pieces to be collected in vials and stored somewhere safe forever. I wanted our house to be a scorched cathedral I wandered through. I wanted it to be mostly air. Your face had her eyes, which was worse. You covered the mirrors and I covered you. We lived like ghosts. Everything was a wound that needed to be burned closed but I wanted to bleed out. I hoped for a curse, for some magic to interfere. Then one night as we lay like rocks in our bed, the clock ticked past midnight and kept going. A hole opened in the space between my exhale and inhale, and deepened. I buried myself in my non-breath and let it close around me. Within those lung-woods, a shadow against a darker shadow, a sense of movement, an edge. A witch, mother as moss, who understood what I had come for. Not death, but a rest no mammal could arrive at with its nerves and blood, its offspring living then not. I felt the witch's hands on my calloused face, my coarsening shoulders, my heartwood spine. Then I didn't. I hadn't for hundreds of years. Beneath our heavy featherbed of soil, we are reaching toward each other. We are tangling without touching. Slow as sap, soft as thread, I am sending you the smell of her hair, her teddy bear, her sheets. You are sending her voice, crackling like lightning at one hundredth the speed. We soak in the patter of her hopping feet, which is painless as rain. We make a wet, inhuman sugar from the syllables of her name.

GLOSSARY OF WHAT I'LL MISS

Autumn, always. The buzz
by which we know the katydid and the fly.

Coral accumulating its slow colonies, the flax
darting bluely through the meadow.

Every evening, the valley is a v
filled with amethyst heat. I was once full of you—

girl who will someday be ghost,
heart that hurts and hurts—

I was once an unscarred peach. But terror
jigsawed my edges until I was sticky as burdock

kernels, clinging to the burlap
legs of every passing catastrophe. Moons ago,

magnolias and jasmine meant *swoon*,
not *imagine a life without them.*

Orange weavers didn't always trail
plumes of their own vanishing through the dusk.

Q is for quiet rooms swelling into disquiet. J
reminds me that by June, the year is already hemi-

sphered, a deflating balloon. My own March
trills somewhere in the field behind me, its song

unraveling. Even you are made of
vanishing, new as you are:

waves of your cells have already died,
xeroxed themselves, and died again. Such magic

yields fewer and fewer miracles. I'll miss the lamb,
zealously. You. The autumn-blooming sweet pea.

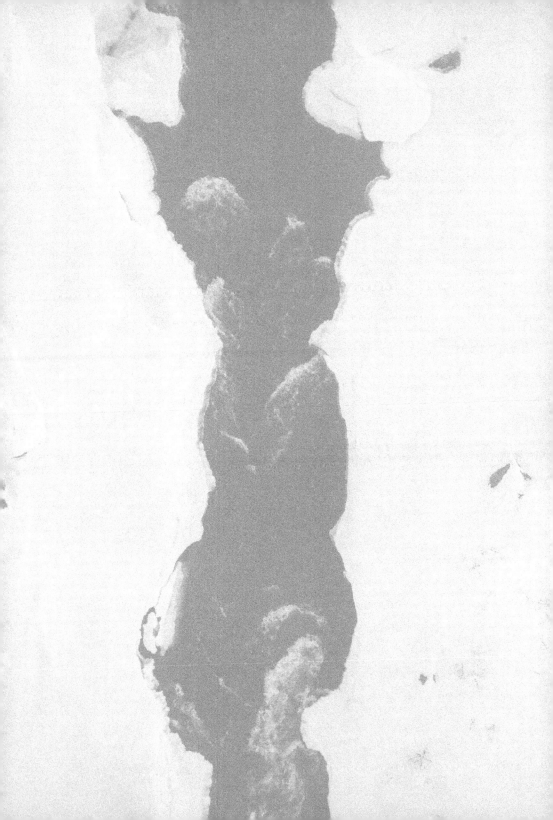

THE NEW FEAR

To say it was like air would be boring,
and it was. There was nothing new about it
except that it was new. It accumulated
in our homes like souvenir shot glasses
or promotional magnets—nothing we noticed
until we couldn't close our cabinets, couldn't find
a clean surface to rest our anxiety on. It pooled
in our urine and our sewers. It ballooned
beneath the skin of rats.
                   New holes gaped
in the ozone layer. Above schools, churches,
movie theaters, new mouths widened and widened
until they ran out of air. But unless they expanded
faster than all our other hole-shaped failures—
the holes in the redwoods, the holes in the ice,
the holes in the elephants' flanks—who cared?
If our pupils were dilated it was because
it was always dark; if our hearts were beating faster
it was because we were always running.
Our blood sugar was so high that our wounds
had stopped healing.
                  The fear was structural
as muscle. Like apples grown inside plastic molds
to resemble hearts or stars, babies were cut out
of us wearing fantastic shapes—grenades,
mandrakes, a stretch of cactuses. They were born
stork-bitten in every helpless place, scarlet and hurt-
looking. We kept them in their rooms, blinds down,
in the half light, all their lives. They grew to the size
of their cribs, no more.

And in that light that wasn't
really light, with our children who weren't really
children, we saw that fear was the organ and the tissue
and the cell, the membrane and the organelle. We saw
no separation between the body and the bullet,
no line between the lung and the water that fills it.
The white letters of dread were invisible against
their surface of snow. There were no words
for what could scare us now.

THE NEW LANGUAGE

After the fires, the plague, the long summers
of green rain, we wanted so badly to touch each other.

Each word was a different arrangement of bodies:
a human body together with an animal body,
or a human body together with a body of water,
or a heavenly body together with a body cavity,
or the body of Christ together with a body bag.

This language was heavier, was more like earthworks—
could, in some cases, be seen from space.

For *tornado*, one body blew on another's pinwheeling hand.
Drought required one human body to backstroke across
another, which pretended to be a desert body's
generous sand.
                The cost of words was volatile.
Though they were always happening, we rarely spoke
of earthquakes (a stack of ten bodies lying on
a writhing eleventh). *Hypercane* took every body
we could find. *Gore* only required pieces.
We needed the sun to shine for *exposure*, needed
the alignment of at least three stars for *fortune*.
For *debris*, three people had to be the glitter,
the toothbrush, and the outlet cover, and one
had to be the baby albatross stomach. We fought
dumbly, grabbing at each other's mouths,
grunting *eat eat eat*.

Agreement was difficult, then
impossible. Down the street, we found four human bodies
kicking the body of a cat and finally understood this
to be a version of *scapegoat*. In the alley, we couldn't read
the two bodies that stood forehead to forehead,
counting each other's blinking.
                                        Some words could only
be said once. *Irreversible* required each participating body
to turn itself inside out. For *zero-sum*, everyone had to agree
to become light at the same time. We were hoping
to save that one for the end, though there wouldn't be
a shape for that pain: the sound of the sun, the sight
of a thought split from its body, the rain like rain.

GLACIER

It is everywhere. It is the water I am trying to teach my daughters to float in. It is the sky I tell them to keep their eyes on. It is the air I tell them to seal in their mouths should they slip underwater. I am a leaky boat, but I am trying to answer their questions. *As deep as thirty Christmas trees. As deep as twenty giraffes standing on each other's backs.* There hasn't been a sea here for seventy-five million years. I cannot explain that number. My daughters' ankles are sinking into the beryl water. No one can float forever. On the map, pushpins skewer patches of icy green like rare moths. I am trying to say it's too late without making them too sad. *It's like how you can't take the blue out of the white paint, like how you can't hear your name and not turn around.* The calving of glaciers is the loudest underwater sound on Earth. I dip my daughters' ears beneath the surface to let them listen. *It's like how you can't put a feather back on a bird, like how the bird won't fit back into its shell.* We step backward into the house. I wring the glacier out of their suits. I wring it out of their hair. I wipe it from their faces, but it is everywhere. It is the storm, it is the drowned harbor, it is the current, it is the bathwater that the baby slurps before we can stop her. The horizon rises. It rains. The glacier hammers the roof, the glacier soaks a corner of the bedroom ceiling, which greens with spores. On the map, the pushpins hover over green air, the green air is a spreading shroud. The storm surges ashore, mercurial and summer-smelling. We are not accustomed to the sea, so we describe it like a sky. The waves are tornado-green and loud. In the water, the polar bears look like clouds.

MELTWATER

barren

:

the valley   which
                                                         had
shrunk

in the

drought   while
the wind

continued   to

glove

us

         with

air

.

        melting

:

                                the

linkage

                  of urgency

and

                      knowledge

, which

contained a sort of memory

.

continuous

:

the   silence

,

                                        The   lifeless
                    Ice   ,

                                                            the
            warm

                        lake   forming   .

P

P is for picture book, the pillow at our backs, my daughter in her Peppa Pig pajamas. P is for peace and peace lily and Peace rose; for *peek-a-boo* and *this little piggy*. I open *Plip Plop Pond*'s flashspun polyethylene pages and point to the polliwogs and lily pads. Let P not be for the Permian Basin and its pipelines and petrochemical plants. Let the phosphorus not proliferate, the pH not plunge. I flip to Paddington, perched politely outside the Lost Property Office, and try not to picture the cruise ships pumping sewage into Peruvian ports. But P is for plague ship. P is for Point Nemo, where de-programmed spacecraft pinwheel into smaller and smaller rain, pepper the waves with paint chips. Around it, the Garbage Patch purls its plastics into pieces smaller than plum pits, smaller than pixels, pinpricks, plankton. P is for plastic, more permanent than permafrost. I open *Each Peach Pear Plum* to spy it hidden in the ptarmigan, the pheasant, in the phthalo blue of the Portuguese man o' war. I read *The Princess and the Pea* and feel the pellets in each layer of the ocean: epipelagic, mesopelagic, past where light penetrates, into the bathypelagic, abyssopelagic, where scientists have found polyester in the molten putty between the Pacific and Philippine plates. P is for the pontoons of Polar Spring, Propel, and Panama Blue. I sing "Baby Beluga" and see pods of pilot whales with pool floaties pretzeled inside their pelvic cavities. I turn the page but it's a palindrome of panic. The petrel preens petroleum from its plumage. The propeller pulps the back of the porpoise. The pressure on my windpipe will not unwrap itself. My daughter has slipped into sleep. I place her outside my arm's parenthesis so she can't feel my pulse pounding. *P is for parachute*, I whisper. *P is for pearl, penicillin, picnic, planetarium, platypus, plink, the pocket-sized pipistrelle, the Ponderosa and its pine beetles.* I turn up the pink noise on her sound machine so she can't hear that P is also the end of *chirp, tulip, kelp, scallop, icecap, sleep.*

DEATHBED DREAM WITH EXTINCTION LIST

Lately, my dreams have been more dead
than usual. They have always been a little dead,
but only around the edges. Or the deadness
has been a dimple on the dreamscape:
a little sweet, a little fermented, a little vegetal.
Appalachian yellow asphodel, the dream says,
and its sunny stars shine, exuberant and dead
and loudly so. The bluebuck lowers its blue face
into them. The cryptic treehunter carries
a dwarf mantis orangely into a tree. Because
the dream is so dead, there is no difference
between the land and the sea. The eelgrass limpet
could easily be mistaken for a mountain pebble,
the forkshell for a shelf fungus. Because the dream
is so dead, there is no difference between moss
and my breath. The golden toad clambers across
the cloud forest of my face. I have followed
the speckled trail of Himalayan quail feathers
and now I am on a beach that is also a mountain
that is also, somehow, the scrubby backyard
of my childhood home. The Indefatigable
Galápagos mouse is here, which seems unlikely
as anything. I hadn't thought to see the Japanese sea lion
again, or for the first time. I've heard that most people die
within one day of having a dream like this, in which
I am packing my suitcase full of Kauaʻi ʻōʻō mating calls.
In the forested canyons of being dead, they can
finally be answered. Most people die within a day
of waking from this dream, but if life on Earth

were a day, we have only been awake for one minute
and fifteen seconds of it. Long enough to erase
the large sloth lemur and the Mariana mallard
and eighty-three percent of everything else.
On balance, it's unnatural to be living. A statistical
impossibility. *Extinct* means *extinguish* means *quench*,
but what mouth is so thirsty for our deadness?
What could hold the Navassa curly-tailed lizard
as it curls its tail in alarm? What could hold
ten million species? The Old English bulldog,
for example, or the aquarium full of phantom shiners
gleaming like the northern lights. It is already
flamboyantly night. The space between the stars
is startlesome as the eyes of the Queen of Sheba's gazelle.
I recognize the Rodrigues night heron by its unwary
amble. I too had thought myself unassailable,
buoyant with time. O night soft as sea mink,
everything's going to be fine. O Tasmanian tiger,
not even one hundred years gone. What kind of sponge
is this dream, that it can soak up so much time?
What happens when it's squeezed? My knees have become
upland for the upland moa. My hips are mottled
by the Vegas Valley leopard frog. I don't know
how an entire forest has sprouted inside my lungs,
but I have been cooperative, and the leaves
of the woolly-stalked begonia have been so gentle.
My cells rumble beneath the plod of the Xenoceratops,
which honestly seems too big to have vanished.
My heart is itchy. I would like to place it in a cooler body.
I would like to place it in a den of Yunnan lake newts
and let their red spines outshine my blood,
though everything is already shining from the edges

in and closing the doors behind it. There has been
some confusion. I meant for the dream to end,
but not while I was inside it. I have mistaken
the dream's deadness for my own skin, my breathing
for the shaky song of the Zulu ambush katydid.

IF ANYONE ASKS

By now I have so many and so much / that fortune can't do harm
NIOBE, *THE METAMORPHOSES*, OVID

Do not compete with gods, and do not boast
THE METAMORPHOSES, OVID

I do not wake up buzzing with happiness.
In fact my bed is full of wasps. I have been stung

everywhere tender. I have not had fun
in a long time, maybe in ever.

My blessings do not run over and also
I have none. My sink is leaking.

My sink is running over with wasps.
They have carried off all my sugar.

See how poor I am, how luckless, how unshapely
my head from which no hair falls in waves.

I have no children to speak of,
no robes sewn with threads of gold,

no robes. I am a patch of dirt, a glass
of vinegar, a bony goose among fat others.

I am an unworthy enemy, small and mean.
In fact calamity has already been and gone,

its arrows still clean. I do not need to play dead.
Not even death would want to play with me.

IN SORROW THOU SHALT BRING FORTH CHILDREN

but still we called you forth
ALICIA JO RABINS, "BABIES IN THE APOCALYPSE"

i.

It was like this: an unearthly wind overtook me, knocked
down a stand of trees, broke open a bright blue
space in the woods of me. Or call the wideness violet,
something warm and future, a color more like the inner reaches
of the body. I woke from myself, cupped within sorrow's hands.
In that blood-light, I was a sudden nebula of desire.

ii.

From inside its fog, I tried to describe this new desire.
As a taste: seawater. As a sound: a woodpecker's knocking.
As if anything could live there, I put my hand
to my chest and melted a sorrow-sized patch in its blue.
Who would walk on this beach, with its waves always reaching
to be ice? When I pulled my hand away, it held a bunch of violets.

iii.

I welled, swelled. I was full of hyacinths, full of African violets,
full of peach blossom and peony. Sorrow and desire
mixed at my roots. I was a black dirt rainforest, reaching

through my own mist for passionflowers, knocking
stalks of sugarcane against my shins until they were blue.
Bees could have made honey just by landing on my hands.

iv.

The Beehive Cluster, the Honeycomb Nebula: deep space is a hand
full of sweetness and sting. The light of the newest stars is ultraviolet,
invisible, hot as your fingers on my palm. In astronomy, a blue-
shifted body is one borne toward the observer. Like desire,
but volition-less, less human. I thought your arrival would knock
all the sorrow from me instead of increasing its reach.

v.

I have eaten blueberries beyond blue. I have reached,
thirsty, into thicket after thicket, scooping saltwater hand-
fuls to my mouth. Miraculous, sorrowful fruit. The world knocks
but I am locking all the doors. I am devouring the sugared violet,
the blackberry fool. I am trying to forget their richness, my desire
a fruit I will someday need to turn away from, my mouth still blue.

vi.

This would be sorrow: to say no. It is autumn. There are still blue-
birds, but few. The dew point is high but falling. Soon we will reach
the last warm day. I am teaching you something about desire
without wanting to. I have you listen for the woodpecker, the hands

of the clock ticking past fullness. I point to the sky that is violet,
then less violet, then black. In the darkness, the knocking

of my heart is bright blue, a color I cannot uncouple from desire.
Here you knock. Here your sunlit hand reaches,
points at my flowering sorrow. *Look,* you say. *A violet.*

POEM WITH NO CHILDREN IN IT

Instead, the poem is full of competent trees,
sturdy and slow-growing. The trees live on a wide
clean lawn full of adults. All night, the adults grow
older without somersaulting or spinning. They grow
old while thinking about themselves. They sleep well
and stay out late, their nerves coiled neatly inside
their grown bodies. They don't think about children
because children were never there to begin with.
The children were not killed or stolen. This is absence,
not loss. There is a world of difference: the distance
between habitable worlds. It is the space that is
unbearable. The poem is relieved not to have to live
in it. Instead, its heart ticks unfretfully among the trees.
The children who are not in the poem do not cast shadows
or spells to make themselves appear. When they don't walk
through the poem, time does not bend around them.
They are not black holes. There are already so many *nots*
in this poem, it is already so negatively charged.
The field around the poem is summoning children
and shadows and singularities from a busy land full
of breathing and mass. My non-children are pulling children
away from their own warm worlds. They will arrive
before I can stop them. When matter meets antimatter,
it annihilates into something new. Light. Sound. Waves
and waves of something like water. The poem's arms
are so light they are falling upward from the body.
Why are you crying?

MELTWATER

long
  is

      the

                name

           of
            the   century.

      small

           is

a   child

  in

           side

              of

            it

            .

on the

black

  Earth

          ,

some   say

memory is

the most distressing thing

.

we scramble

in   to

the crater

of   Its

silence   .

THE FUTURE

The body is lined with it, like a nest,
like the down the eider plucks from her breast

until her nest is a gray mist weighed down
by five sea-green eggs. At the end of each season,

only one duckling will survive to fly
away. This is an average. On any given day,

all of the eggs may hatch, all of the hatchlings
may freeze. The gulls may cruise in rings

above the nesting colonies, the polar bear
may not surge ashore. The female eider

can lay eggs for eighteen years, more or less.
Without wanting to, I do the math. She will lose

seventy-two chicks before she dies, those numbers
traded against her own long years by nature's

calm calculus. There is only so much life
to go around. It isn't like a flame, whose belief

in itself is enough to burn a forest down.
Instead, we have been given one

bolt of cloth to be shared. The choice is
in how you shear it. I say *choice*

but of course it's not. It's a vast, organic machine
running like static behind everything; the gene

doesn't want anything, doesn't want, doesn't
exist except by cosmic mistake. *Accident*

means *to move toward a fall*. And so they fall
and fall through time, carelessly, like a carnival

ride whose switch is stuck in the "on" position.
I would like to die before losing any children.

In fact, there is no reason for me to be alive anymore.
Having borne my code into the future,

even if only by another lifetime, I could not matter
less. Eider ducklings enter the water

motherless, will dive for mussels on their own
just one day after hatching. If they escape starvation,

the gulls, the cold, when will the dying begin?
When do the cells start to multiply or weaken?

The eider's scientific name is *Somateria mollissima*:
the softest body. My own is already less terra firma

and more open water, more unmooring, more
losing. I may have already begun to rupture

invisibly, my cells may have already begun
their unwinding. Time picks us up then sets us down

a little further on, pulses through us like a wave.
Sometimes it seems as if the eggs survive

just to keep the nest from blowing away.
I have stayed, even though it makes me prey

to worse things than freezing wind or gulls.
I am mostly glad we are not wild animals.

I am mostly glad about most things, even
the future, even though I know that broken

shells may float on its waters. I need to think
that the eider doesn't grieve the breaking.

MELTWATER

an

      early

mourn

ing.

child,   you are

a memorial   at the site of

                        our   story
                        on

            the   black

Earth
,

I   say

we

are

the

Most

irreversible

thing   .

:

future: to become another thing:
to feel the air ring

with songless, sudden
weight: water will soften

every saltless land:
inside the silk gland,

the spider's unspun gossamer
sits liquidly like early summer:

church bells anneal into time:
bird bones melt beneath the lime

trees: skin moves toward itself
across a sore: half

a night away, a war
is renamed into another war:

half of my cells become
yours: your name

becomes a better universe:

THE EMPTY UNIVERSE

The stars pull away from each other

the stars pull the sky apart

or everything comes apart and the stars
expand into what that means

there is only free-falling in space

there are many small gravities

we are only ever falling into the orbit
of the nearest body

for months my hands have been falling away
from my heart, which must no longer have the mass
to attract them

sometimes I find my feet in the other room

every morning they are more and more numb

I almost wrote *number* but their deadness
is not quantifiable

all my failures are similarly intangible
but constant: dark dependable ingredients
to build a universe around

I cannot keep my body together

I cannot, this night, stop myself
from listening to my daughter wail
and wishing she were less like herself
therefore less like me

even though the space between us
has only grown since she appeared

her body falling toward the surgeon's
stronger hands, my own body suddenly
ninety-five percent of its former mass
and dropping

until it reaches this night

where I feed the heels of my hands
into the black holes of my eyes

until they are shredded brightly
into a web of plasma

the most generous form of matter in the universe

the least like me, who pushes her hands
deeper and deeper into her eyes' sea

until it blooms with blue-green algae
swarms of fireworms swimming through

a darkness that is never fully dark
a silence that is never fully silent

the curtain of the universe falls between us
a gray stutter

that touches my face through my hands
like rain through a cloth

here   *here*   it says

and my legs, my heels, my thighs hear
and return from their far dimensions

which I do not deserve

just as I do not deserve to be the signal
my daughter's voice homes on
the skin she finally hushes against

here   *here*   is the grace

we suffer the empty universe for

XYZ

The year yellows. The yolk of yesterday's sun lazes in the yard, piled beside the yew and yarrow, the zucchini vine that never flowered, the waxy Zenobia. It sprawls like yarn, a yawn that won't be swallowed back into summer's mouth. I am zombie-eyed, zephyr-minded, would sleep until the next equinox if I could, would relax my heart until it stopped. The cold rises through the thorax and into the larynx. The autumn haze is heavy and thick as a smashed yam. Through it, pollen floats like yeast. It is hard to follow the wren's pitch and yaw, its yammering. Yearling, heir of my X, you are full of the reflex to live. I am hexed, cannot be coaxed to thrive. *Zygote* means *yoke*, the zipping of two bodies together, the axes on which are plotted a galaxy of Xs and Ys. Somewhere in that matrix is your syntax of chromosomes. You are a black box, a maze of invisible zigzags, beyond exegesis. The toadflax freezes from radix to apex. The ilex is evergreen but untouchable, the fuzz of some animal transfixed in its thorns. I think about extinction, the unidirectional vortex of time, read all the obsolete entries of the dictionary: the codex ywrit in lampe blacke; the yale ykoweryn by phlox up to its helixed horns; whelps ydreynt; the mouse in grasse by the fox ylaid; the phoenix from its sooty nest yborn ad infinitum. I don't care for eternity, its violence boxed and distributed into months. I don't care for the zodiac, twisting back on itself like a zero. It only reminds me that your star is not fixed, that no stars are, that all measurements—azimuth to zenith—measure only emptiness. Even the sphinx knew that time is the most vexing puzzle. I envy the zebra distributing its name endlessly among the zebra fish, the zebra mussel, the zebra finch. Back in the garden, the drizzle glazes into ice. A bronzed apple thuds, a broken yo-yo. I cannot say *no*. I allow myself to be yanked back up, exhausted. Seized by the topaz sky and the breeze through it. By *yes*, by you.

NOTES

Each poem titled "Meltwater" is an erasure of Lacy M. Johnson's "How to Mourn a Glacier," first published in the *New Yorker* on October 20, 2019, and reprinted with generous permission of the author. No word appears in more than one erasure—in other words, the size of the pool decreases with each erasure.

"Deathbed Dream with Extinction List" was shaped by the following sources: Jan Hoffman, "A New Vision for Dreams of the Dying," *New York Times*, February 2, 2016; J. Scott Janssen, "Deathbed Phenomena in Hospice Care: The Social Work Response," *Social Work Today* 15, no. 6 (November/December 2015): 26; Damian Carrington, "Humans Just 0.01% of All Life but Have Destroyed 83% of Wild Mammals—Study," *Guardian*, May 21, 2018.

ACKNOWLEDGMENTS

"Meltwater" [Ice stretches between us and history], "Glacier" [The room was huge and cold], and "Glacier" [Zero degrees] were reprinted in *Dark Mountain*: Issue 20—Abyss (2021).

"Glacier" [It is everywhere] won the 2022 Montreal International Poetry Prize.

Grateful acknowledgment is made to the editors of the following journals, where these poems, sometimes in earlier versions and under different titles, first appeared:

> *32 Poems*: "In a Land Where Everything Is Already Trying to Kill Me, I Enter a New Phase of My Life in Which It Would Be Very Bad If I Died"
> Academy of American Poets, Poem-a-Day: "O," "Poem with No Children in It"
> *The Account: A Journal of Poetry, Prose, and Thought*: "Meltwater" [we are joined], "Meltwater" [long is the name], "Meltwater" [an early mourning]
> *Beloit Poetry Journal*: "Glacier" [The room was huge and cold]
> *Blackbird*: "In a Land Where Everything Is Trying to Kill You, I Teach You to Be an Autotomist," "Glossary of What I'll Miss," "Deathbed Dream with Extinction List," "The Future"
> *Copper Nickel*: "If Anyone Asks," "At the End We Turn into Trees"
> *Couplet Poetry*: "In Sorrow Thou Shalt Bring Forth Children," "The Empty Universe"
> *Descant*: "Meltwater" [Ice stretches between us and history], "Meltwater" [we land in a cold valley], "Meltwater" [O world]
> *Good River Review*: ":," "Poem That Cries Wolf"

Great River Review: "Glacier" [We waited behind the velvet rope],
    "Glacier" [Zero degrees], "Apotropaei," "XYZ"
Grist: "M"
Image Journal: "The New Fear"
Literary Matters: "Hunger," "You Will Soon Enter a Land Where
    Everything Will Try Trying to Kill You"
Los Angeles Review: "The Child Puts Apples into the Mouth of the
    Tree"
The Louisville Review: "Primer"
Montreal International Poetry Prize Anthology 2022: "Glacier" [It is
    everywhere]
Ninth Letter: "In a Land Where Everything Is Trying to Kill Me, I
    Consider Letting It"
On the Seawall: "Starling"
RHINO: "Metamorphosis with Milk and Sugar"
Sierra: "P"
Southeast Review: "The New Horticulture," "More Rabbits," "The Sun,
    the Ship"
Washington Square Review: "The New Language"

Thank you to the McKnight Foundation for awarding me a 2020–2021
fellowship that enabled me to write some of these poems.

Major gratitude to the Milkweed crew for their generosity of time and spirit as
this book came together.

Thank you to Laura Bylenok, Sara Eliza Johnson, Michael Lavers, and Daniel
Lupton for reading drafts.

Daniel Lupton

CLAIRE WAHMANHOLM is the author of *Redmouth* and *Wilder,* which won the Lindquist & Vennum Prize for Poetry and the Society of Midland Authors Award for Poetry, and was a finalist for the 2019 Minnesota Book Award. Her poems have appeared in *Ninth Letter, Blackbird, Washington Square Review, Copper Nickel, Beloit Poetry Journal, Grist, RHINO, Los Angeles Review, Fairy Tale Review, Bennington Review, DIAGRAM, The Journal,* and *Kenyon Review Online,* and have been featured by the Academy of American Poets. She lives in the Twin Cities.

milkweed
EDITIONS

Milkweed Editions, an independent nonprofit publisher, gratefully acknowledges sustaining support from our Board of Directors; the Alan B. Slifka Foundation and its president, Riva Ariella Ritvo-Slifka; the Amazon Literary Partnership; the Ballard Spahr Foundation; *Copper Nickel*; the McKnight Foundation; the National Endowment for the Arts; the National Poetry Series; and other generous contributions from foundations, corporations, and individuals. Also, this activity is made possible by the voters of Minnesota through a Minnesota State Arts Board Operating Support grant, thanks to a legislative appropriation from the arts and cultural heritage fund. For a full listing of Milkweed Editions supporters, please visit milkweed.org.

Interior design by Tijqua Daiker and Mary Austin Speaker
Typeset in Arno

Arno was designed by Robert Slimbach. Slimbach named this typeface after
the river that runs through Florence, Italy. Arno draws inspiration from a
variety of typefaces created during the Italian Renaissance; its italics were
inspired by the calligraphy and printing of Ludovico degli Arrighi.

Printed in the USA
CPSIA information can be obtained
at www.ICGtesting.com
JSHW021519010424
60353JS00003B/80

9 781639 551019